Daniel

Ellen Caughey

Illustrated by
Ken Landgraf

BARBOUR
PUBLISHING, INC.
Uhrichsville, Ohio

© MCMXCVIII by Barbour Publishing, Inc.

ISBN 1-57748-366-9

Published by Barbour Publishing, Inc., P.O. Box 719, Uhrichsville, Ohio 44683 http://www.barbourbooks.com

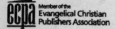
Member of the
Evangelical Christian
Publishers Association

Printed in the United States of America.

Daniel

THE KING'S MAGICIANS.

1

The temperature outside the massive stone palace of King Nebuchadnezzar must have been at least 110 degrees—but inside you could hear teeth chattering and knees rattling. After bowing nervously in front of the throne, the king's magicians now stood as if they were freezing cold. In truth, they were scared to death.

King Nebuchadnezzar, ruler of the empire of Babylon, had just awakened from a very troubling sleep. "I have had a dream that troubles me and I want to know what it means," he declared from his mighty perch.

In a sweeping movement, Aliabad, the chief magician (or astrologer, as he was known), bowed once again before the king. "O King, live forever!" he cried, giving the standard greeting to the king. "Tell your servants the dream, and we will interpret it."

Stroking his mangled beard, Aliabad tried to look like he knew what he was doing. He and his fellow astrologers had succeeded in pleasing the king in the past. But just about anyone could flatter the king with a phony horoscope or fine fortune. Aliabad had a feeling this time was different.

All eyes were glued on Nebuchadnezzar.

"Oh, you astrologers who think you know everything! This is what I have decided: If you do not tell me what my dream was and what

"I HAVE HAD A DREAM THAT TROUBLES ME."

it means, I will have you cut into pieces!" The king's voice echoed throughout the palace chamber.

The astrologers had never heard such a request! How were they to know what the king had dreamed? As they gathered together several yards from the throne, their hands were moving up and down, their eyes were rolling, their heads were shaking in unison, and their wild whispers sounded like a beehive just discovered by a bear.

King Nebuchadnezzar flashed the trembling astrologers a wicked grin. "Don't think I don't know what you're doing—you're trying to buy time! So let me tell you again, in case you didn't hear right the first time. If you tell me the dream, I will know you can tell me what it means. If not. . ." Closing his eyes, the king plopped a giant fig into his mouth.

Once again a shaking Aliabad threw himself on the floor, his robes flying behind him. "There

ALIABAD THREW HIMSELF ON THE FLOOR.

is not a man on earth who can do what the king asks! No one can tell the king what he dreamed—except maybe the gods, who do not live with us." (Aliabad was speaking of gods that men had created to explain the changes in weather and the seasons, and why good and bad things happen to people.)

At that, the king's face turned deep red and he rose from his chair, flinging the fig stem onto the ground. "How dare you," he began slowly, his anger rising. "Today every one of you will die!" Then, turning to a servant who was trying to look invisible, he added, "And while you're at it, find Daniel and his friends. Put them all to death!"

The swooshing sound of his silk robes as the king strode out could not compete with the terrified cries of Aliabad and the others.

THE SWOOSHING SOUND OF HIS SILK ROBES....

DANIEL AND HIS THREE FRIENDS WERE KNOWN THROUGHOUT THE PALACE.

2

Daniel and his three friends, Hananiah, Mishael, and Azariah, were well known throughout the palace of King Nebuchadnezzar. Just three years before, in 605 B.C. (more than six hundred years before the birth of Jesus), the four of them had been brought to Babylon from Jerusalem in the land of Judah. Because Nebuchadnezzar (and his armies) had conquered Judah, he had the right to bring back to his country whatever Jews he wanted to be slaves.

But the king was a wise ruler, and he wanted to remain one for years to come. So he selected certain young men of Judah—handsome, well educated, and from noble families—for special training. One day, after years of learning to speak the Babylonian language and to read ancient books, especially those on mathematics and astrology, these men would give the king advice on important matters, like predicting the future or interpreting dreams.

Twelve-year-old Daniel and his friends were among those chosen and then carted away—500 miles to the east of Jerusalem—to the luxurious palace of the great Nebuchadnezzar in the city of Babylon.

From Jerusalem, the caravans of Nebuchadnezzar headed north, across the rugged mountains of Syria and Aram to reach the bustling

TWELVE-YEAR-OLD DANIEL AND HIS FRIENDS WERE CARTED AWAY.

city of Aleppo. The course was then set to the east, finally encountering the great Euphrates River at the city of Tiphsah.

And from Tiphsah, the captives from Judah followed the river's southeast path for many months until they finally reached the city of Babylon, the capital of the Babylonian empire.

As the four friends passed under the Ishtar Gate, the main entrance into the city, they couldn't help staring up. "Have you ever seen a city like this?" Daniel asked.

Mishael couldn't help noticing the lions and dragons created by the yellow and brown colors of brick that decorated the Ishtar Gate. From a distance, the gate had seemed to be made entirely of purple. "Are there really dragons and lions in Babylon?"

Daniel made a funny face at his friend. "Oh, Mishael. Didn't the rabbis tell you about all the strange gods they worship here? I think the

"HAVE YOU SEEN A CITY LIKE THIS?"

dragon is the symbol of their god Marduk—"

Hananiah interrupted. "And the lion stands for the goddess Ishtar, is that correct?"

Azariah summed up their situation perfectly. "Well, we are not in Judah anymore. That's for sure!"

On their first complete morning in the palace, the four friends found themselves seated on colorful, overstuffed pillows, trying to memorize the Chaldean alphabet, the one used by all Babylonians. But that wasn't all they were having trouble getting used to. Upon entering the king's service, they had each been given a new Babylonian name.

Daniel would now be called Belteshazzar, after the Babylonian god Bel; Hananiah would be known as Shadrach, or one "inspired by the sun-god"; Mishael was now called Meshach, which meant "who is comparable to Shak," another name for the goddess Venus; and Azariah would

EACH WAS GIVEN A NEW BABYLONIAN NAME.

forever be addressed as Abednego, or a "servant of the fire god."

Tall for his age, Daniel stretched his long arms over his head and gave a frustrated yell. "I have had it! Who among us likes these names?"

Silence.

Then Hananiah had an idea. "Let's use our old names when we're together. When we're with the king, well, I will have to get used to being a sun god."

Azariah's eyes opened wide. "Does that mean I will be able to breathe fire out of my mouth?"

Daniel leaned over and punched his arm in response. "Let's be serious for a minute. Just in case we forget what our old names mean, I'm going to write them somewhere, in our old language. We may be here a while."

On separate lines on a small piece of papyrus, Daniel wrote the following:

Daniel, "God is my judge."

ON A PIECE OF PAPYRUS, DANIEL WROTE, "GOD IS MY JUDGE."

Hananiah, "whom God hath favored."

Mishael, "who is comparable to God?"

Azariah, "whom God helps."

Daniel then motioned for the four of them to stand. He read aloud what he had written on the papyrus. Then he tucked the crinkled scrap inside his belt. "Today, right now, let us make a promise before God. No matter what happens to us here in Babylon, no matter if we never see our families in Jerusalem again, no matter what—we will serve the one and only God, the Most High God, El Elyon."

As the four friends put their hands together, Daniel said, "As long as God is on our side, we will not be afraid."

Just then, loud footsteps came to a halt outside their room, and Ashpenaz, the chief of King Nebuchadnezzar's court officials, entered grandly.

"Uhhh-ummm! Begging your pardon, young sirs, but lunch is served!"

"BEGGING YOUR PARDON, YOUNG SIRS, BUT LUNCH IS SERVED."

Barely visible under the weight of the enormous golden tray was Ashpenaz's young assistant, Melzar, who managed to set his burden down without too much difficulty. There on the king's tray was more food than Daniel, Mishael, Hananiah, and Azariah had ever seen—tall urns filled with wine, fruits and nuts of all kinds, figs and olives, and sticky looking cakes dripping with honey. But what caught the boys' attention was the head of a pig surrounded by thick, juicy slices of pork and lamb!

"Well?" Ashpenaz broke the silence. "The king himself has requested that you eat what he eats. Such an honor for such young men!"

"I am afraid we cannot eat anything on this tray," Daniel said, his eyes meeting Melzar's for a minute before facing Ashpenaz. "It is not that we don't appreciate everything the king is doing for us, but—"

WHAT CAUGHT THE BOYS' ATTENTION WAS THE HEAD OF A PIG.

Ashpenaz interrupted him immediately. "But what?" His bushy black eyebrows seemed to meet in the middle of his wrinkled forehead.

Smothering his grin, Daniel thought he was looking at one very active, furry caterpillar. "You see, as Jews, my friends and I must not eat this food. If we take one bite, we will be going against everything our parents taught us, and everything God wants us to do."

The laws of the Jews, given to Moses from God, were very specific about what foods, and what animals, could and could not be eaten.

Azariah nodded his head. "Take that pig—no Jew can eat that!"

Mishael, Hananiah, and Daniel were almost laughing at the thought of what their mothers would do to them if they even considered such a meal.

The boys couldn't explain to Ashpenaz and Melzar every reason why the king's food was

MISHAEL, HANANIAH, AND DANIEL ALMOST LAUGHED
AT THE THOUGHT OF SUCH A MEAL.

unacceptable. But any grown-up Jewish person would have known that the first serving of Nebuchadnezzar's food was offered to idols, not to the one true God. And the first portion of wine was poured out on an altar used to worship these idols.

Ashpenaz was silent for a moment. He seemed to be considering what the boys said. "King Nebuchadnezzar, long may he reign, has given you this food, and you reject it all! You know, you aren't the only boys the king is preparing to be his advisers. What if the king sees you and thinks you don't look so good? And then he finds out you aren't eating his food? What do you think the great King Nebuchadnezzar will do to me?"

Like the goblets on the golden tray that rattled back and forth, Daniel and his three friends seemed a little nervous. But not one made a move toward the tray.

"WHAT DO YOU THINK THE GREAT KING NEBUCHADNEZZAR WILL DO TO ME?"

"Lizard got your tongues, or should I say, your stomachs? My fine friends, should you refuse the king's food, my head—and not that pig's— might be on that tray!"

At that the four boys cried out together, "No, no, no!"

Daniel then stood and faced Ashpenaz and Melzar. He took a deep breath and tried to appear older than his twelve years. "Please, I have an idea. Give us nothing to eat but vegetables and nothing to drink but water for ten days. Then compare how we look with the other boys who have eaten the king's food."

Ashpenaz and Melzar paced the length of the oriental carpet, their heads bowed, their voices muffled. Finally, Melzar spoke. "Ten days only, Belteshazzar, then we shall see."

For ten days, Daniel, Mishael, Hananiah, and Azariah drank only water and ate only vegetables, while the other young men in the king's

FOR TEN DAYS THEY DRANK ONLY WATER AND ATE ONLY VEGETABLES.

training feasted on rich and exotic foods. And they prayed three times a day, as was their custom, facing west in the direction of Jerusalem. They prayed that God would give them strength.

Now the moment had arrived. Who would look healthier?

When Daniel and his friends joined the others in the courtyard of the palace, Ashpenaz and Melzar peered carefully at the group. Then Melzar whispered in Ashpenaz's ear and the older man smiled knowingly.

"Water and vegetables for everyone!"

Daniel, Mishael, Hananiah, and Azariah looked so much better than the other boys that now everyone would eat the way they did—by order of the king. That night as he said his prayers, Daniel thanked God for giving him the courage to take a stand for his faith. God had led him to this strange country, to this magnificent palace, and to this curious king for a reason.

DANIEL PRAYED THAT GOD WOULD GIVE THEM STRENGTH.

ARIOCH, A TOWERING MUSCULAR SOLDIER. . . .

3

The determined footsteps of King Nebuchadnezzar's chief officer echoed down the stone hallways of the palace fortress. But Arioch, a towering, muscular soldier, was not at all eager to do what the king had ordered. While other guards had been sent to find Daniel and his three friends, he alone had been ordered to put the astrologers to death. They were a slimy bunch, those magicians, and Arioch could imagine what crazy things they would say to him: "A curse on your family dog!" "May your skin turn green and your hair fall out!"

Then Arioch thought about Daniel. Somehow, no matter what Arioch said to Daniel, Daniel had a way of answering him that made everything seem all right. The word around the palace was that Daniel, Mishael, Hananiah, and Azariah had ten times the wisdom of the other young men in training—not to mention the astrologers!—and something more. The word around the palace was that some god was on their side, the one Daniel simply called God.

Shaking his head, Arioch thought to himself how Daniel would need his God now—more than ever. And then Arioch saw him, turning the corner just ahead, his face almost covered up by the book he was reading.

"Daniel! Just the person I wanted to see," Arioch boomed out, voicing a lie.

"DANIEL—JUST THE PERSON I WANTED TO SEE."

"Arioch, I didn't see you coming," Daniel apologized.

Arioch breathed a huge sigh.

"Something is wrong, terribly wrong, isn't it?" As usual, Daniel knew what to say.

"Yes, my young friend. I may as well tell you." So Arioch retold in great detail the troubled sleep of the king and the king's strange request of the astrologers. Finally, the king's chief officer revealed what the king had in mind for Daniel and his friends.

But Daniel did not look worried. "Why did the king order all of us to die?" he asked calmly.

Arioch tried to explain but he could see Daniel was already forming a plan.

"I must see the king right away!" Daniel announced, then turned, almost running toward the king's chambers. Arioch raised his hand to stop him but it was too late.

An hour later, Daniel was seen leaving the

"I MUST SEE THE KING RIGHT AWAY!"

king's chambers to find Hananiah, Mishael, and Azariah. He was alive and well, but in a hurry. What had happened between Daniel and the king?

Piecing together bits of information, Arioch was able to tell the story. "I can't believe he said this but he did," he told a group of fellow guards later over dinner. "Unlike those silly magicians who said they could only tell what the dream means, Daniel is going to do the impossible, my friends. He saved his life and the lives of his friends by asking for time—to tell the king the dream *and* what it means. I only hope he knows what he's doing!"

Candles flickered around the darkened room as Hananiah, Mishael, and Azariah listened closely to Daniel. "We have only one answer. We must ask God to tell us the mystery of King Nebuchadnezzar's dream. Only God knows what the king dreamed."

"WE MUST ASK GOD TO TELL US THE MYSTERY OF NEBUCHADNEZZAR'S DREAM."

For the next several hours, the friends prayed and prayed, often lying face down on the cold stone floor. Sometimes they cried out loud, and sometimes only soft whispers could be heard. Then Daniel opened his eyes.

"Praise be the name of God forever and ever!" he shouted. "Wisdom and power are His! He reveals deep and hidden things! I thank and praise You, the God of my fathers—"

"Daniel, Daniel, did God speak to you? What did He say?" Hananiah asked eagerly.

"My friends, I must see Arioch at the first light. God has made known to me the dream of the king."

Arioch was smiling broadly when he greeted Daniel outside his room. "So, you can do what the king has ordered?"

But Daniel did not return his smile. "Do not kill the astrologers, Arioch. Take me to the king."

As they approached King Nebuchadnezzar's

"SO, YOU CAN DO WHAT THE KING ORDERED?"

throne, the king's eyes were closed as if he were asleep. But then his arm shot up, causing Daniel and Arioch to freeze in their steps. "Well?" the king's voice boomed. "Are you able to tell me what I saw in my dream and what it means?" One eye opened and fastened on Daniel.

"Not I, King Nebuchadnezzar, but God has revealed the mystery of your dream!"

Daniel swallowed, then continued. "God has shown King Nebuchadnezzar what will happen in days to come. I do not possess greater wisdom than others; I am only being used by God so that you will understand your dream."

The king nodded, and a slow smile crept across his face.

Daniel cleared his throat. "In your dream you saw before you a large statue, an enormous, awesome statue! The head was made of pure gold, its chest and arms were silver, and its stomach and thighs were made from bronze.

"GOD HAS REVEALED THE MYSTERY OF YOUR DREAM."

The legs of the statue were iron, but the feet and ten toes were made partly of iron and partly of baked clay."

The king's smile quickly faded. As he gulped the wine from his massive silver goblet, he motioned Daniel with a flick of his hand. "Go on, go on."

"Suddenly, from out of nowhere, a rock not cut by human hands appeared and smashed the statue, breaking it to pieces! And then the wind swept the pieces away."

Daniel paused a moment, then continued. "But the rock that came from nowhere became a huge mountain and filled the whole earth. This was your dream."

The king nodded again, his eyes fixed on Daniel. "Yes, that was my dream. But what does it mean? Did your God tell you that, too?"

"The head of gold is you, King Nebuchadnez-zar. The God of heaven has given you power

THE KING NODDED AGAIN, HIS EYES FIXED ON DANIEL.

over men and women, animals and birds. He has made you ruler over them all. But after you, other kingdoms will arise, kingdoms not nearly as grand as yours, even one made of iron, that will conquer everything it desires. Finally, the toes of the statue, made of iron and baked clay, are ten kings who will rule on the earth many years from now. But this kingdom will be partly strong and partly weak. At that time, the God of heaven will set up a kingdom on earth that will never be destroyed or conquered by other peoples, a kingdom that will last forever. That kingdom is the rock not cut by human hands, a rock out of a mountain."

The king's chambers were so quiet even the flies refused to buzz. Looking the king squarely in the eyes, Daniel said, "The great God has shown the king what will take place in the future. The dream is true and the interpretation is trustworthy."

..."THE GREAT GOD HAS SHOWN THE KING
WHAT WILL TAKE PLACE IN THE FUTURE."

At that, King Nebuchadnezzar stood and ran toward Daniel, falling on his face before him. Gasps could be heard all around—no one had ever seen a king as mighty as he worship another human being, especially a young man like Daniel!

"Surely your God is the God of gods and the Lord of kings!" Nebuchadnezzar cried. He then struggled to his feet. "Today I appoint you, Belteshazzar, ruler over the province of Babylon and ruler over all the astrologers of the palace."

"You are very generous, King Nebuchadnezzar," Daniel answered. "I just have one favor to ask. . . ."

And on that same day, King Nebuchadnezzar appointed Hananiah, Mishael, and Azariah administrators over the province of Babylon. They would travel around the kingdom while Daniel remained at the palace. [1]

"SURELY YOUR GOD IS THE GOD OF GODS AND LORD OF KINGS!"

That night, Daniel could not sleep. Rising from his mat, he went up to the roof of the palace to gaze at the stars. And he was not disappointed. Against the inky blanket of night, delicately positioned, were what seemed like millions of precious diamonds. *And to think God knows the name of each star,* Daniel thought to himself.

"Why am I surprised?" he then asked no one in particular, for the guards were positioned a distance away from him. That day, God had performed an incredible miracle, one no man could do. That day, God had revealed himself to a powerful king, but a king who still believed God was one of many gods. "Why, God? Why?" he questioned the sky.

And then one answer came to him: God was not finished with the proud Nebuchadnezzar.

"TO THINK GOD KNOWS THE NAME OF EACH STAR."

"YOU REMEMBER IN MY DREAM, ALIABAD, HOW I WAS THE HEAD OF GOLD?"

4

Even though many weeks had passed, King Nebuchadnezzar could not get his latest, most troubling dream out of his mind. And even though Daniel had interpreted the dream to his satisfaction, the king was still restless.

"You remember in my dream, Aliabad, how I was the head of gold?" King Nebuchadnezzar said to his astrologer one afternoon.

Nodding for the umpteenth time, Aliabad

forced himself not to yawn. "Yes, O King, gold, more precious than all metals! And a kingdom of gold, grander than any empire!"

Stroking the first of his many chins, the king continued pacing his chamber. "My point exactly! But how will the world know? I must tell the world!"

Then, suddenly, the king collapsed on his throne and began laughing and clapping his hands. "I've got it, oh, this is so good! Why didn't I think of this before? But then, only *I* could have thought of such a lasting tribute, such a salute, such a statue!"

Aliabad turned his back on the king as if to cough, then rolled his eyes at the servants behind him. "Statue, did you say, King Nebuchadnezzar? Like that of a god?"

"Yes, yes, but so much better," said the king, sounding slightly displeased with Aliabad's limited thinking. "Picture this: a statue made

THE KING BEGAN LAUGHING AND CLAPPING HIS HANDS.

entirely of gold, larger than any statue in Babylon! A statue set on a hill so that all peoples may know there is one Nebuchadnezzar, one Babylon—a statue that all peoples must bow down before and worship. Only in Babylon can such a statue exist!"

"Only in Babylon" was not an exaggeration —at least not to the million or so Babylonians, and perhaps an even greater number outside Nebuchadnezzar's kingdom. For only in Babylon were there two of the seven wonders of the world, the magnificent "hanging gardens," and the amazing high wall that surrounded the city.

The gardens, which were built by Nebuchadnezzar to please his wife, Amytis, were not gardens at all, but a huge hill. This man-made hill rose to a height of three hundred fifty feet and had trees planted on either side of a ten-foot-wide staircase. Then there was the city wall, eighty-seven feet high and three hundred

THE GARDENS WERE BUILT BY NEBUCHADNEZZAR TO PLEASE HIS WIFE.

fifty feet wide—so wide that four chariots could ride side by side!

And now "only in Babylon" there would be a gleaming gold statue set high on the plain of Dura, a statue that would measure ninety feet tall and nine feet wide. A statue no one could miss!

A day of dedication was declared for King Nebuchadnezzar's statue and all of Babylon gathered for the celebration. All the king's astrologers were there, led by Aliabad whose nose was held so high he nearly stumbled as he walked in the procession. Following them were the royal judges, governors, and treasurers.

And then there was King Nebuchadnezzar himself. Seated on a golden throne—"My favorite color!" he declared—the king then gave the signal to begin the ceremony.

"O people of Babylon," declared the king's

"MY FAVORITE COLOR!" HE DECLARED.

herald (the one who makes royal announcements), "as soon as you hear the sound of the horn, flute, harp, and other instruments, you must fall down and worship the statue of gold. Those who do not will be thrown into a blazing furnace!"

Silence greeted the herald's terrifying pronouncement. This blazing furnace was really a huge industrial furnace used by Babylonian workers for baking bricks and smelting metals. Set outdoors, the furnace had a large opening at the top from which flames could be seen shooting up—hungry, devouring flames. To be thrown into the blazing furnace meant instant death.

And then the music began—beautiful melodies and grand, stirring chords—music fit to worship a king. And all the people fell down immediately and worshipped the golden statue of King Nebuchadnezzar.

THEN THE MUSIC BEGAN.

All the people, that is, except Mishael, Hananiah, and Azariah. [2]

Lying on his stomach, Aliabad turned his head, and from the corner of his eye he could see them standing. His usual smile—kept in place for royal occasions—turned into a sneer. Poking another astrologer, he motioned to the three men who had refused to obey the king's command. "Look at them!" Aliabad hissed between his teeth. "Who do they think they are?"

"But they—and Belteshazzar—saved our lives, Aliabad. We can't turn them in!"

"What you say is true. But I cannot just sit here and watch how they treat Nebuchadnezzar! The king has given them more riches than you could ever want. Maybe if we just call this little incident to the king's attention, he will reward us, his most loyal servants—don't you think?"

When the music ended Aliabad eagerly struggled to his feet, hurriedly straightening his robes.

HIS USUAL SMILE TURNED INTO A SNEER.

First, he must inform the other astrologers of this act of disobedience and then. . .then he would lead them to the throne of King Nebuchadnezzar.

At last Meshach, Shadrach, and Abednego will know their rightful places in the king's palace, Aliabad thought to himself. *As ashes in his fireplace!*

After waiting for the crowds of people to bow one last time before the king, Aliabad had his opportunity. "What a day, King Nebuchadnezzar! And the golden statue and the music—why, not much could be better!"

"Not much, Aliabad? I thought my day was perfect! Was a musician out of tune?" The king was still smiling but a look of concern had creased his forehead.

"No, no, nothing like that. I mean, it's not nothing, it's just. . ."

"SPEAK UP!" the king's voice thundered and all eyes rested on Aliabad.

"SPEAK UP!" THE KING'S VOICE THUNDERED.

Aliabad came closer to the king, as if what he had to say was very private. "There are some Jews to whom you have given much power in Babylon, Jews who pay no attention to you, Jews who do not fall down and worship your statue!"

"Shadrach, Meshach, and Abednego? They did not worship the statue?" The king's voice was trembling with anger.

"I did not want to be the one to tell you, O King, but I felt someone should," Aliabad answered, managing not to smile.

"BRING THEM HERE AT ONCE!"

When they were brought before the throne, the three friends looked puzzled. His face almost purple with rage, the king was clearly upset at them.

"Is it true, Shadrach, Meshach, and Abednego, that you do not worship the statue of gold? That when you heard the music you did not fall down

"IS IT TRUE, SHADRACH...?"

at once? IS THAT TRUE?" The king's finger pointed at them was shaking.

Shadrach, or Hananiah, spoke for the group. "O King, we serve only one God, the God of heaven, and He has commanded that we must not serve other gods. For that reason, we cannot worship the statue of gold."

"You tell me this, then. What god will be able to rescue you from the fiery furnace? Will yours?" Nebuchadnezzar glared fiercely at Shadrach.

"If we are thrown into the furnace, the God we serve is able to save us. But even if He does not, that is all right, too, because it is His will that we die."

"No, it is MY WILL that you die, and die today!" the king bellowed. Turning toward his nearest servant, the king ordered the furnace heated seven times hotter than usual. And then he commanded that Shadrach, Meshach, and

THE KING ORDERED THE FURNACE HEATED
SEVEN TIMES HOTTER THAN USUAL.

Abednego be thrown into the hungry flames.

Dressed in flowing robes and pants, with turbans covering their heads, Hananiah, Mishael, and Azariah were bound with ropes and led up a flight of steps to be thrown into the blazing furnace. But because King Nebuchadnezzar had ordered the furnace to be made hotter than usual, at the top of the steps, flames could be seen leaping several yards into the air. Anyone who came close would surely be burned to death.

And so it was that the servants who led the three men up the steps were killed instantly by the flames just as they threw the three men into the furnace.

Moments later, King Nebuchadnezzar went to a window built into the side of the furnace. His hand went to his mouth and at first no words came out. "Weren't only *three* men thrown into the fire?" he gasped.

FLAMES COULD BE SEEN LEAPING INTO THE AIR.

"Certainly, O King," one servant answered.

"But I see four men walking around in the fire, men not bound by ropes! And they are all alive! The fourth man, he looks like a son of the gods." Nebuchadnezzar immediately started to climb the steps. "Come out, Shadrach, Meshach, and Abednego, come out! Now I know that you are servants of the Most High God."

When the three men heard the king's voice they came out of the fire, only to be met by a crowd that couldn't believe their eyes. There were Shadrach, Meshach, and Abednego, alive and well! Not a hair on their heads had been singed by the fire, their robes were not burned, and not one man smelled like he had been near a roaring fire.

Nebuchadnezzar then rushed to their sides, grabbing their hands in his.

"Praise be to the God of Shadrach, Meshach,

"NOW I KNOW THAT YOU ARE THE SERVANTS OF THE MOST HIGH GOD."

and Abednego!" the king cried. "He has sent his angel to be with you in the furnace and rescued you. What kind of God do you serve? You who were ready to die rather than bow down before any other statue!"

Turning around to face the people, the king cleared his throat. "Today I make a new command to my people. If anyone says anything against the God of Shadrach, Meshach, and Abednego, that person will surely die. No other god can save like their God!"

At that, Aliabad and his fellow astrologers made a quick exit from the scene, and were not seen for many days. But Shadrach, Meshach, and Abednego—Hananiah, Mishael, and Azariah—were still in a daze. They had been saved again by their God, saved again for a reason.

That day the king promoted Hananiah, Mishael, and Azariah, giving them even more important titles than before. And that night, the

"NO OTHER GOD CAN SAVE LIKE THEIR GOD!"

three men prayed for Nebuchadnezzar, that he, too, would worship the God that saves—before it was too late. [3]

THE THREE MEN PRAYED FOR NEBUCHADNEZZAR.

THUNDERHEADS HUNG JUST ABOVE THE PALACE.

5

Thunderheads hung just above the palace of Nebuchadnezzar waiting to burst open with welcome rain. But the stormy weather had little to do with the king's lack of sleep.

"I haven't seen the king so upset about a dream since—" one servant whispered to another, only to be interrupted by Aliabad, who now entered the chambers.

"Yes, don't remind me about that dream, at

least not at this hour! And anyway, that was years ago," the astrologer added.

"Aliabad, is that you? Come here, please come here," came the strangely quiet voice of the king. The king was sitting hunched over on his throne, his head in his hands. "I need you to call all of the magicians here—at once."

Aliabad did not have time to hide the surprise from his face. Bowing quickly, he turned and left the chambers, and returned a short time later with every magician he could find. Everyone except Daniel. "Tell us your dream, O king, and we will provide our usual excellent interpretation," Aliabad stated grandly, bowing again to the floor.

But a short time later the astrologers left the king's chambers, their shoulders slumped and their feet dragging, now reduced to whispering insults to each other.

"That kind of dream is your specialty, Habib, not mine!"

"TELL US YOUR DREAM, O KING."

"You have no specialty, Sarik, except eating perhaps!"

"Eating? You could give a pig nightmares!"

Aliabad cut short the two bickering astrologers and motioned the group to look down below. Running across the courtyard was Daniel, his robes flying, being taken by Arioch to the chambers of Nebuchadnezzar.

"Why is the king calling *him* now?" Aliabad whispered bitterly.

"As if you don't know," Sarik said under his breath.

"But as the *chief* astrologer—" Aliabad rolled his eyes as if to belittle Daniel's promotion over him—"why wasn't Belteshazzar called first? This time I feel our 'friend' Belteshazzar will not have a ready answer for the king." A sly smile spread over Aliabad's face.

"Maybe the king doesn't really want to know what this dream was about," Habib suggested

ALIABAD MOTIONED THE GROUP TO LOOK DOWN BELOW.

wisely. "I mean, that would explain why he called us first."

Shrugging their shoulders, the astrologers returned to their rooms, secretly hoping their "services" wouldn't be required anytime soon.

Daniel found the king in much the same way as the astrologers had minutes earlier. *This dream is worse, much worse than the last,* Daniel thought to himself. *God in heaven, please give me wisdom and courage!*

"Belteshazzar, chief of the magicians, I know that the spirit of the holy gods is in you. I know that no mystery is too great for you," Nebuchadnezzar began.

Immediately Daniel was troubled. Even though everyone in the palace knew that he had been promoted to chief of the magicians, the spirit of one God, not many, controlled his life. Obviously, the king had not learned much in his past encounters with the God of Daniel,

"I KNOW THAT NO MYSTERY IS TOO GREAT FOR YOU."

Hananiah, Mishael, and Azariah.

Maybe, thought Daniel, *this time God will change the stubborn king's heart.*

The king looked terrified as his eyes roamed the room. He then motioned Daniel to come closer, as if anyone else overhearing this dream might spell disaster. "Here is my dream, then. Interpret it for me.

"I was lying on my bed and there before me stood a tree, an enormous, strong tree, the top branches of which seemed to touch the sky. The leaves of the tree were beautiful and there was more fruit hanging from the branches than you could imagine. Under the tree, animals found shelter and birds rested on the mighty branches."

The king paused to catch his breath and then continued. "Then I saw an angel coming down from heaven! And this angel, he ordered the tree cut down, all the leaves stripped off, and the

"THERE BEFORE ME STOOD A TREE."

fruit scattered everywhere. Then the animals ran away and the birds flew off to find another tree."

"Was there nothing left of the tree?" Daniel asked.

"I was just getting to that. The angel then ordered that the stump and the roots of the tree be left in the field and bound with iron and bronze. As if speaking to a person, the angel said to the stump that it would live with the animals, and that its mind would be changed from that of a man to the mind of an animal for seven years."

"Is that the dream?" Daniel asked.

"Not quite. By then there were many angels in the sky and all they could say was that God is ruler over the kingdoms of men. God gives to anyone He wishes, and He also sets over His people the lowliest of men. That is the dream, Belteshazzar, the dream none of my astrologers could interpret."

"THERE WERE MANY ANGELS IN THE SKY."

Daniel's face had lost its color. Feeling he was about to faint, he sat down—and then said nothing for almost an hour. King Nebuchadnezzar could wait no longer.

"Belteshazzar, do not let my dream or its meaning upset you so much."

"My king, if only the dream were meant for your enemies and not for you!" Daniel cried. "But the tree you saw, the beautiful, healthy tree whose branches reached the sky, that tree is you, O King. You have become great and strong, and your empire reaches to distant parts of the earth."

"And what is so terrible about that, Belteshazzar?"

"But you are also the stump and the roots of the tree. You will be driven from your kingdom and will live with the wild animals. You will eat grass like cattle and be drenched by the rains from heaven."

"YOU WILL EAT GRASS LIKE CATTLE."

"But my kingdom is so powerful! How could anyone take this away from me, the great Nebuchadnezzar?" Seizing a bunch of grapes, he plopped several into his mouth at once.

"There is more, my king. Seven years will pass before you—the once mighty king—bow before God. Seven years will pass before you finally believe that God is the ruler over all the kingdoms of men and gives them to whomever He wishes. The roots of the tree were not destroyed for a reason. Your kingdom will be restored to you when you finally believe that only God rules your empire."

"When will this all take place? I can see no armies about to attack, only a thunderstorm."

"I cannot tell. I only know this: Ask God to forgive you for your wicked deeds. Be kind to those who are poor and sick. Maybe then this dream will not come true."

As Daniel left the king's chambers, he glanced

"SEVEN YEARS WILL PASS BEFORE YOU FINALLY BELIEVE THAT GOD IS THE RULER OVER ALL THE KINGDOMS OF MEN."

over his shoulder for a last look at the sleepless Nebuchadnezzar. A larger tray of many varieties of grapes had been placed by his feet, but the king was unaware of it. Servants hovered on either side of him, but the king seemed to ignore them. Fans of peacock feathers held by maidservants swayed up and down to no reaction from the dazed Nebuchadnezzar.

And then a bolt of lightning seemed to slice the room in half, followed seconds later by a crashing boom of thunder—and the cries of a king pleading with his gods.

A BOLT OF LIGHTNING SEEMED TO SLICE THE ROOM IN HALF.

MANY WARS HAD BEEN FOUGHT.

6

With every passing month Daniel watched for changes in King Nebuchadnezzar. But now twelve months had passed—one whole year— and the king was still thinking clearly, still very much in charge of his empire, and, if possible, even more powerful than ever.

Many wars had been fought, and many years had gone by since Daniel had been taken captive and brought to Babylon. And now Babylon was at peace. Life was good for the king, and he knew it.

Nebuchadnezzar had forgotten Daniel's advice, and he had forgotten the words of the angels in his dream: "God gives the kingdoms of men to anyone He wishes and sets over them the lowliest of men."

On this cloudless day, one year after his dream, King Nebuchadnezzar was on the roof of his palace, enjoying the magnificent view of Babylon. And it was a view like no other! The city formed a perfect square, fifteen miles in length on every side, with wide streets and towering buildings. The surging Euphrates River ran right through the middle of the city and under the city walls to the plain, the result of Babylonian engineering.

Positioned between two of the more than two hundred fifty watchtowers on the roof, the king felt safe as well as powerful. And seated beside

IT WAS A VIEW LIKE NO OTHER!

a now graying Daniel, his most trusted adviser, he felt nothing could go wrong with this day. And then a thought came to him, a thought that had to be spoken.

Standing, with his arms outstretched, Nebuchadnezzar proclaimed, "Is not this the great Babylon, built by my mighty power and for the glory of my majesty?"

Nebuchadnezzar's words seemed to hang in the still air. Then a voice was heard, a voice that didn't come from the roof or the city streets below. A voice that came from heaven.

"This is what is decreed for you, King Nebuchadnezzar: Your royal authority has been taken from you. You will be driven away from people and will live with the wild animals. You will eat grass like cattle. Seven years will pass before you say that God rules over the kingdoms of men and gives them to anyone He wishes."

NEBUCHADNEZZAR'S WORDS SEEMED TO HANG IN THE STILL AIR.

Turning to look at the king's reaction, Daniel couldn't believe his eyes. For immediately, the once mighty Nebuchadnezzar had become exactly as the creature described in the dream.

"Help, someone, help!" Daniel yelled to the guards, who nearly dropped their spears when they saw the king.

There on the floor of the roof, still in his robes, was King Nebuchadnezzar, sniffing the ground for food and making growling sounds. Daniel and the guards moved away from him, trying again and again to speak to him, but it was no use. Nebuchadnezzar simply bared his teeth and lashed out at them with his jeweled hand, now more like a paw.

It took several guards to finally move the king down to his rooms. But like the wild animal that he had become, it was impossible to keep the king in one place. When, after many days, the king's wife, sons, daughters, and servants

KING NEBUCHADNEZZAR WAS
SNIFFING THE GROUND FOR FOOD AND MAKING GROWLING SOUNDS.

realized they could not control him, the king was set free in the wilderness outside the city gates of Babylon.

Only the birds and beasts that roamed the desert could observe the changes in the once feared king. His lavish robes had long been torn away and his skin had become as thick as leather. The once glorious mane of hair that had been fit to cushion the crown of an empire now resembled the feathers of an eagle. And his fingernails and toenails—once filed and oiled by adoring servants—looked like the overgrown claws of a bird.

Day after day, week after week, and year after year, Nebuchadnezzar lived the life of an animal. He ate what grass he could find, much like a cow, and his body was washed by the dew from heaven. Living like he had lost his mind, not to mention his beloved kingdom of Babylon, the once proud king kept

THE ONCE PROUD KING KEPT HIS HEAD DOWN.

his head down, looking only for his next meal.

And seven years passed.

The day after seven years had gone by, Nebuchadnezzar raised his eyes to heaven. And immediately God changed his mind back to that of a man. He stood up and stretched out his arms. And then he fell back on the ground.

"O most high God, I praise and honor You, You who live forever! Your kingdom is eternal, lasting from generation to generation. All the peoples of the earth are nothing compared to You. And yes, now I know that You do as You please with the powers of heaven and the peoples of the earth."

And then, wrapping an animal skin about his body, King Nebuchadnezzar started walking back to the city of Babylon. Remembering the stump in his dream, whose roots had not been destroyed, he knew he would sit again on his throne, but not as the same man as before.

WRAPPING AN ANIMAL SKIN ABOUT HIS BODY, KING NEBUCHADNEZZAR
STARTED WALKING BACK TO THE CITY OF BABYLON.

That same day, Daniel was again on the palace roof, staring out at the city but not looking at anything in particular. On the other side of the roof he heard some commotion, the sound of feet running toward him. Turning, he saw one of Nebuchadnezzar's oldest and most trusted servants, holding his sides, obviously out of breath.

"Master Belteshazzar, come quickly! He is back, he is back!"

"Who are you talking about?"

And then Daniel knew. Seven years had passed. He ran down the stairs faster than he had in years, rounding the corners in a flurry, making his way to the king's chambers.

Standing there, in the middle of the room was Nebuchadnezzar. He had on one of his former robes, which was now several sizes too big. His face was deeply tanned but his eyes sparkled. And as he grabbed Daniel's hand, Daniel felt the coarse, rough skin.

AS HE GRABBED DANIEL'S HAND, DANIEL FELT THE COARSE, ROUGH SKIN.

"O King, you are here, just as in your dream!" Daniel said excitedly.

"Yes, Belteshazzar, I have been restored, just as your God—and mine—promised." Daniel was about to say something but the king stopped him. "Please, let me finish. My pride in myself prevented me from knowing God; I now know that. And only God is able to humble those who think they are more powerful than He. Now I just want to spend the rest of my days praising God, and thanking Him for allowing me to serve Him."

And so it was that Nebuchadnezzar continued to reign as king of Babylon until his death. Nobles from near and far sought an audience with him and his reputation and wealth grew with each passing year. But always, he gave praise to God—the God who, after three powerful encounters, had changed his life.

ONLY GOD IS ABLE TO HUMBLE THOSE
WHO THINK THEY ARE MORE POWERFUL THAN HE.

DANIEL AND HIS FRIENDS WERE SIMPLY OLD MEN.

7

The palace of Babylon had become a lonely place for Daniel. Many years had passed since Nebuchadnezzar ruled the empire, and many years had passed since a godly king sat on the throne. Now in the year 539 B.C., few in the palace remembered the courage and faith of Daniel and his three friends, Hananiah, Mishael, and Azariah. Or even knew who they were.

Daniel and his friends were simply old men, all

around eighty years old, who somehow, some-time, had earned the respect of a long-ago ruler.

Would they ever be allowed to return home to Jerusalem? Or had God planned for them to live out their days here? Until recently, they had no reason to hope. But now there was talk through-out the palace that the armies of the Medes and Persians were nearing the famous city walls of Babylon.

Seated together in one of the palace's many gardens, the four friends were troubled. *Had anyone told the new king about Nebuchadnez-zar's first dream?* they wondered. *The one of the statue?* Nebuchadnezzar was the head of gold, but after him came the kingdom of Medo-Persia, the Medes and the Persians.

The great kingdoms of Media and Persia lay almost directly to the east of the kingdom of Babylon. In 550 B.C., Cyrus the Great of Persia had conquered Media, and now, together with

THE ARMIES OF THE MEDES AND PERSIANS
WERE NEARING THE FAMOUS CITY WALLS OF BABYLON.

General Darius the Mede, he turned his attention to Babylon. Since the death of Nebuchadnezzar, Cyrus knew Babylon was not the force it once was. And if he conquered Babylon, the world could be his very soon.

"Do you think one of us should warn King Belshazzar? Or even King Nabonidus when he returns? Maybe if Belshazzar prayed to God, this war might be delayed," suggested Hananiah.

"God has not directed me to do that," Daniel answered slowly. "And we all know that God is not welcome in the king's chambers—at least, not yet."

"You are right as always, my friend," Azariah said. "And what is welcome in the king's chambers. . ." With sadness in their eyes, they all shook their heads.

Two kings, father and son, now shared the throne of Babylon. The father, King Nabonidus, who was married to the daughter of

TWO KINGS, FATHER AND SON, NOW SHARED THE THRONE OF BABYLON.

Nebuchadnezzar, ruled the empire outside the city of Babylon. Belshazzar, his son, ruled the city from the throne in the palace.

Even though King Belshazzar was the grandson of Nebuchadnezzar, he had little in common with the former king. Instead of keeping Babylon secure from its enemies, he spent his time entertaining at lavish parties, drinking too much wine, and worshipping his many idols—idols of silver, gold, wood, and stone.

Although he was aware that Babylon would soon be at war, Belshazzar made a typical entrance, skipping into his chambers while humming a silly tune, only to meet a sea of dark and serious faces. The faces of his military advisers.

"Why so sad today? Haven't you heard—but surely you were invited—tonight I'm giving my biggest party yet!" Belshazzar could not keep from giggling. He had obviously been

"TONIGHT I'M GIVING MY BIGGEST PARTY YET!"

drinking and it was early in the day.

"King Belshazzar, the news of the Medes and Persians is not good. In fact, spies report that our enemies may attack Babylon tonight," one adviser stated.

"If only I were on a first-name basis with what's-his-name. Or who's the other one?" Lost in thought, the king began twirling a lock of his short, curly hair.

"Cyrus, you mean? The king of Persia?" One adviser stared amazed at the king.

"And Darius, the general of the Medes?" another added.

"Yes, him and him. I mean, they're welcome to join us, but perhaps that would be a bit much!" And at that Belshazzar dissolved into fits of laughter.

"King Belshazzar," another adviser began, "perhaps tonight is not the best night for your, er, celebration. Our spies report the Medes and

"KING BELSHAZZAR, THE NEWS OF THE MEDES..."

Persians have the best weapons and more soldiers than—"

"STOP! How dare you ruin my party! Now
go, all of you. I need to speak to the chefs and
wine stewards about more important matters."

That night in the great banquet hall of the
palace, the tables were set for a thousand guests.
Silver plates and gold trays gleamed in the
candlelight, not to be outdone by the sparkling
jewels worn by all present. Only the wealthiest
of Babylon were there, and each one wanted to
be noticed.

As King Belshazzar sipped from his oversized
wine goblet, he was pleased with the way the
party was going. But then a thought crossed his
mind, a thought that would not go away. These
guests were used to being served on the finest
silver and gold. Tonight, the night of his grand-
est party, he would not disappoint them.

After whispering an urgent order to the servant

ONLY THE WEALTHIEST OF BABYLON WERE THERE.

by his side, the king sat back in his chair. Why hadn't he thought of this before?

Later, as the servants of the king paraded into the hall, each carrying a tray, gasps could be heard from the guests. For on every tray, polished to a rare sheen, were the most magnificent gold goblets they had ever seen.

"King Belshazzar, where have you been keeping these? They are exquisite!" exclaimed one noble seated at the king's table.

"And what are these writings on the goblets? From what distant land did these come?" another guest inquired.

The king was beside himself with pride. What a brilliant move this had been to bring in the goblets stolen from the holy temple in Jerusalem— goblets brought to Babylon seventy years ago and never used until now.

Standing, Belshazzar watched until each guest had his own goblet, and each goblet was filled

EACH GUEST HAD HIS OWN GOBLET.

with wine. "Drink up!" he cried out, almost laughing. "And as we drink, let us make a toast to the gods of Babylon, the gods who have given us so much!"

As all the guests sipped the wine from the rare golden goblets, out of nowhere the fingers of a human hand appeared. No arm, no body, no legs, no head—just the fingers of a human hand, floating in the air.

Dancing amid the shadows cast by the candlelight, the mysterious hand traveled between the tables of the banquet hall. When the hand neared the walls, the shadows the fingers themselves created were the scariest of all. The hand seemed far larger than any human hand, and far more dangerous.

The room fell silent, except for the nervous rattling of goblets and silver on the tables and the gasps that escaped the open mouths of the bejeweled guests. One servant dropped his

OUT OF NOWHERE, THE FINGERS OF A HUMAN HAND APPEARED.

tray and scurried from the hall. Several women fainted and dropped to the floor from their seats, sending other servants hurrying to their aid.

Even so, all eyes were fastened on the mysterious hand and fingers, and what they would do next.

Then, on the plaster wall behind the king, the fingers began to write a message—a message that consisted of four words. And then the hand disappeared.

Belshazzar sat frozen, his face the color of ashes. But under the table his knees began knocking together.

When he finally raised himself to stand, his legs would not support him and he nearly collapsed to the floor, grabbing the table for balance. "Send in my astrologers immediately!" the king ordered, after clearing his throat several times. "Whoever can tell me what these words mean will be clothed in purple and have

BELSHAZZAR SAT FROZEN.

a gold chain placed around his neck. Furthermore, that person will be made the third highest ruler in the kingdom!"

But when the astrologers examined all four words of the message in great detail, they could not begin to tell the king what the words meant.

At that moment King Belshazzar's mother, Queen Nitocris, the daughter of Nebuchadnezzar, entered the banquet hall. Looking every inch like the mother of a king, with her graying hair piled high on her head and her gown of lavender silk, Nitocris walked slowly toward her son, her back straight. While she nodded her greetings to a select few of the nobles she passed, she clearly had not come to join the party.

"My son, the king, I pray to the gods that you will live forever! You look so pale, but there is no reason to be afraid," she said to Belshazzar. "There is a man in your kingdom—in the palace —who has the spirit of the holy gods in him.

THE ASTROLOGERS COULD NOT BEGIN TO TELL
THE KING WHAT THE WORDS MEANT.

In the time of your grandfather, this man was found to be as wise as the gods. In fact, Nebuchadnezzar appointed him chief of all the astrologers."

"His name, Mother? Do you remember his name?" The king was impatient as always.

"Ah, yes, I do indeed. My father called him Belteshazzar, but his Hebrew name was Daniel. He could interpret dreams, explain riddles, and solve the most difficult problems. You must call for Daniel."

Snapping his fingers, the king ordered that Daniel, whoever he was, be found immediately and brought to the banquet hall. *This Daniel was probably some ancient creature who once had a gift,* Belshazzar thought to himself. Of course, he had to send for him—or lose the respect of all the nobles at the party. His own mother had recommended Daniel, after all.

And then Daniel was led inside the hall. Still

"YOU MUST CALL FOR DANIEL."

a tall man with perfect posture, his white hair flowed in the air as he walked briskly toward the king and bowed before him. The king looked into the piercing blue eyes of Daniel, and then looked away. His grandfather had not been wrong about this man.

THE KING LOOKED INTO THE PIERCING BLUE EYES OF DANIEL.

DANIEL COULD NOT HELP NOTICING THE
ABUNDANCE OF SILVER AND GOLD AROUND HIM.

8

Upon entering the banquet hall, Daniel could not help noticing the abundance of silver and gold around him. The silver plates and serving utensils, the golden trays heaped high with rich foods —the same dishes he and his friends had rejected!—and the bracelets, earrings, rings, and necklaces adorning all the nobles and their wives.

And then his eyes traveled to the golden goblets filled with wine, the rare goblets never before seen in Babylon. Daniel's eyes filled with tears —and then his fists became clenched with anger.

These goblets had been stolen by Nebuchadnezzar from God's temple in Jerusalem. These goblets were only to be used by the high priests to worship God. These goblets were holy!

To make matters far worse, these goblets were being used to drink from—and to toast the false gods of Belshazzar and the Babylonians. *God can wait no longer,* Daniel thought to himself. *God has to show His power!*

Now face to face with Belshazzar, Daniel looked straight into his eyes. The eyes of a coward. The eyes of a man who thinks only of himself and his riches and his pleasures.

"Are you Daniel, one of the captives my grandfather the king brought to Babylon from Israel?" Belshazzar began.

"I am he, O King," Daniel answered.

"I have heard that the spirit of the gods is

THESE GOBLETS WERE ONLY TO BE USED BY THE HIGH PRIESTS.

in you and that you are very wise. Perhaps you can still be of use to me, the grandson of Nebuchadnezzar. . . ."

Daniel said nothing. Clenching and unclenching his fists, he simply stared into the darting eyes of this desperate ruler.

"Out of nowhere fingers appeared and began writing on this wall, and then they disappeared," the king continued, motioning to the wall behind him. "My astrologers, who possess the finest minds for thousands of miles, have already examined this extraordinary message and none of them can tell me what it means."

Daniel turned his attention to the wall behind the king. There was other writing on the wall as well, words praising King Belshazzar, as was the custom of the day. But the four words written by the hand of God were still clearly visible to him:

Mene, Mene, Tekel, Parsin

DANIEL TURNED HIS ATTENTION TO THE WALL BEHIND THE KING.

"If you can tell me what these words mean," the king went on, repeating himself, "you will be clothed in purple, and a gold chain will be placed around your neck. Furthermore, you will be made the third highest ruler in the kingdom."

A pained look crossed Daniel's face. "You may keep your gifts for yourself—or give them to someone else. I will tell you what the writing means without a reward."

Gasps and whispers could be heard throughout the hall, and then silence. Sitting on the edge of their seats, the guests waited breathlessly for the strange, white-haired wise man to speak. Belshazzar eased himself into his padded chair.

"The Most High God, the God of heaven, gave your grandfather Nebuchadnezzar great power and splendor. Because of all that God gave him, your grandfather was a mighty and feared ruler. Those he wanted to put to death, he put to death;

"I WILL TELL YOU WHAT THE WRITING MEANS..."

those he wanted to save, he saved. But when he started to think too much of himself, when he became filled with pride, God took away his glory. Do you remember what happened to your grandfather, O King?"

Daniel's history lesson was beginning to have an effect on King Belshazzar. The king knew that his grandfather had lost his mind. Was that going to happen to him, too?

"Yes, I have heard the stories," the king answered quietly. Then he laughed nervously. "Who hasn't?"

"Stories are sometimes made up and sometimes true. But what happened to your grandfather, the mighty and feared Nebuchadnezzar, was God's plan! Your grandfather was driven away from people and given the mind of an animal. He lived with the wild donkeys and ate grass like cattle. And his body was washed with the dew from heaven—until he worshipped

"DO YOU REMEMBER WHAT HAPPENED TO YOUR GRANDFATHER, O KING?"

the Most High God! Only God rules over the kingdoms of men and sets over these kingdoms anyone He wishes," Daniel said, pausing to catch his breath.

"You may have heard the stories, King Belshazzar, but you have not learned anything from them. Instead, you have set yourself up against the God of heaven!"

The banquet hall suddenly was transformed into a beehive, as anxious voices competed with each other, echoing off the walls of the room. *These nobles are only pretending to like King Belshazzar,* thought Daniel as he gazed from table to table. *As soon as they think he's going to be deposed from power, how quickly they are ready to follow someone else.* But Daniel was not finished with the sad and scared looking king. Not yet.

Looking only at the king, Daniel continued. "You had the goblets from God's holy temple in

"YOU HAD THE GOBLETS FROM GOD'S HOLY TEMPLE."

Jerusalem brought to you tonight, to you and your nobles, so you could drink your wine and toast your gods—gods made from gold, bronze, iron, wood, and stone—gods that cannot see or hear or understand!" Daniel almost spit the words from his mouth.

The king seemed to sink even lower in his chair.

"But you did not honor the God who holds your life in His hands. And for that reason, God sent the fingers that wrote on your wall."

All eyes were now on the message, the four words that no one could interpret:

Mene, Mene, Tekel, Parsin

"The message, as you know, is easy to read: 'Mene, mene, tekel, parsin,' or numbered, numbered, weighed, and divided. 'Mene, mene' means that God has numbered the days of your king-dom and He has brought it to an end. 'Tekel' says that you have been weighed on the scales by God and found to be evil. And finally,

"YOU DID NOT HONOR THE GOD WHO HOLDS YOUR LIFE IN HIS HANDS."

'parsin'—your kingdom will be divided and given to the Medes and Persians."

Oddly enough, at that moment the king stood and placed on Daniel's shoulders the purple robe. Around Daniel's wrinkled neck, Belshazzar placed a heavy gold chain. And then in front of the thousand nobles, he promoted Daniel to third in his kingdom.

Daniel had made his wishes known to King Belshazzar. He did not want to be rewarded for what he did not—and could not—do. Only God could interpret dreams; only God could send fingers to write on a wall; only God could tell a king when his reign was over.

Even though he accepted the king's luxurious gifts, Daniel did not stay at the party. And even though Daniel had warned Belshazzar that the end of his kingdom was here, the party continued. Wine flowed from giant casks and into the golden goblets as the king

BELSHAZZAR PROMOTED DANIEL TO THIRD IN HIS KINGDOM.

and his guests strayed even further from the will of God.

Outside the palace, however, the clear thinking of the Medes and Persians was about to pay off. A plan had been hatched days earlier to change the course of the Euphrates River, the river that flowed under the city walls of Babylon. By stopping the flow of the river, the riverbed under the wall would eventually dry up.

Tonight, the night of Belshazzar's celebration, the riverbed was pronounced completely dry— and that meant everything. The armies of the Medes and the Persians could enter Babylon *under* the famous wall instead of trying to overtake it, a feat that would have been almost impossible.

As loud laughter rang from the palace porticoes in the early morning hours, the troops led by Darius the Mede and Cyrus of Persia completely surrounded the palace. The city was

THE TROOPS LED BY DARIUS THE MEDE...
COMPLETELY SURROUNDED THE PALACE.

theirs—except for the king and his family.

Their swords waving in the air, the soldiers ran into the banquet hall, sending the drunken nobles sprawling on the floor. Those who could still stand weakly tried to run away, but they did not get very far. Goblets crashed to the floor and food went flying as the soldiers made their way to the king.

But King Belshazzar put up little fight. He was captured easily and taken away to be killed. Later, King Nabonidus would also surrender to Cyrus the Great.

Belshazzar's days had indeed been numbered, his deeds had been weighed, and now his kingdom of Babylon was no more. The golden head of the image in Nebuchadnezzar's first dream had been toppled, as another of Daniel's prophecies came true.

As Daniel prayed in the early morning hours, again facing Jerusalem, he wondered if his years

THEIR SWORDS WAVING IN THE AIR,
THE SOLDIERS RAN INTO THE BANQUET HALL.

in Babylon were over. *Dear God, will I be sent home at last?* he prayed. *Or can You still use an old man like me?*

"DEAR GOD, WILL I BE SENT HOME AT LAST?"

DARIUS CALLED DANIEL TO HIS CHAMBERS.

9

The answer to Daniel's prayer came much sooner than he expected. Word of Daniel's powers— "the power of the Most High God," Daniel always corrected—had spread quickly around the Medo-Persian empire, and that included the new king who sat in the palace of Babylon.

Soon after General Darius the Mede had been appointed king of Babylon by Cyrus the Great, he called Daniel to his chambers. Darius had come up with a new plan to rule his portion of the empire and he wanted Daniel, with all his wisdom, to play a significant role. "I want you to know, Daniel, that I will not take no for an answer. Yes, you are older than my other advisers, but you have proven yourself, more than anyone else, capable of a high position in this kingdom."

Daniel couldn't believe his ears after all those years when no one knew him!

"I am honored to serve you, King Darius," Daniel replied.

"Then listen, for here is my plan: The kingdom of Babylon will be divided into one hundred twenty provinces to be governed by one hundred twenty satraps (that is to say, princes). These one hundred twenty satraps will report to three presidents, and those presidents will report back to me, as king. Daniel, I would like you to serve as one of the three presidents."

"I WILL NOT TAKE NO FOR AN ANSWER."

Daniel was aware that the king was studying his face for his reaction. *Surely this must be God's plan,* Daniel thought to himself. *Only God could put me in this position!*

"Again, I would be honored to serve you in whatever way you desire," he answered.

"Good, that's settled then. You will receive further instructions in the days to come. I know you will serve me well, Daniel, just as you served Nebuchadnezzar and Belshazzar during their reigns."

In the months that followed, Daniel did not disappoint King Darius. Time and again, the satraps who reported to Daniel returned to their provinces amazed at his decisions and his wisdom. He settled all disputes fairly and never held grudges against anyone. If the satraps failed to collect the necessary taxes, for example, Daniel always gave them a second chance, and even a third, to prove themselves.

DANIEL SETTLED ALL DISPUTES FAIRLY.

Daniel's performance as president of Babylon was about to be rewarded. As he entered the king's chambers, Daniel faced a beaming King Darius, whose smile stretched from ear to ear. Daniel could not help noticing that standing around the throne were the other two presidents as well as several satraps. But their smiles were only polite—and forced.

"Daniel, Daniel, the honor of your presence is desired!" the king began warmly.

Daniel bowed slowly before the throne.

"You have performed your duties as president to the best of your abilities, which is to say, you have a most excellent spirit. Most excellent! And so today I am pleased to tell you of my future plans for you. Daniel, I am arranging to put the entire kingdom under your control. No longer will you serve simply as a president. You will rule over all presidents and all satraps!"

Again, Daniel scratched his ear to make sure

"I AM ARRANGING TO PUT THE ENTIRE KINGDOM UNDER YOUR CONTROL."

he had heard correctly. "I am without words, O King. I will be pleased to serve you however you desire."

"Then say no more!" the king cried, clapping his hands. "I'll start to make the necessary arrangements. The rest of you may go now, except Daniel. I need to ask your opinion on some pressing matters."

Shooting a glance at the presidents and satraps as they left the chambers, Daniel felt strangely troubled.

Their heads bent and their hands behind their backs, the presidents and satraps moved slowly down the broad pillar-lined hallway of the palace. "We cannot talk here," whispered Tobruk, one of the presidents, as he eyed one of Darius' guards.

"Meet at my home at sunset," Abbad the satrap suggested. "We have much to discuss!"

That evening, the candles in Abbad's home

"MEET ME AT MY HOME AT SUNSET."

burned low as the men weighed many plans. Plain and simple, they were jealous of Daniel. They wanted what he had, especially the power and position that come when one is highly thought of by the king. And if they could not achieve that—and it was obvious that right now they could not—they would find a way to bring Daniel down.

"Abbad, you check how he keeps track of the money of his provinces. Any mistakes and we would have an instant case," Tobruk advised.

"Yes, money is the place to start. Besides, as far as we know, Daniel has never married, he has never been found to be drunk or foolish, and he has never lied to anyone. All he does is read, study, and pray to his God, the Most High God he calls Him," Abbad said.

Tobruk scratched his chin, deep in thought. "Maybe that is the key to our Daniel," he said with an evil glint in his eye.

"YES, MONEY IS THE PLACE TO START."

Days later, the group of presidents and satraps met again in the home of Abbad.

"Upon checking all the records Daniel has kept I have yet to find a single mistake. Every single shekel can be accounted for, my friends. Daniel is a man the king could trust."

"I was afraid of that," Tobruk stated. "So we go to plan B. We will create a new law—a law that goes against the law of the God of Daniel!"

Again the candles burned low that night in the home of Abbad as the small group of presidents and satraps quickly wrote the new law. Too much time had passed already, they decided. They must see the king early in the morning, perhaps before he was fully awake!

With Tobruk leading the way, the group entered the king's chambers the next day, bowing as low as they could before a sleepy-eyed King Darius. "O King, live forever!" Tobruk began, sounding the usual greeting. "The royal

BOWING AS LOW AS THEY COULD GO...

presidents and satraps have all agreed that you should sign a new law that all peoples should obey, starting immediately." Tobruk hoped the lie of this statement was not too obvious.

"Law? This early in the morning? But what is so pressing that I must make such a decision now? Surely this can wait, perhaps until Daniel sees it." The king tried to focus on the group before him.

The presidents and satraps looked at one another with alarm. Abbad then stepped closer to the throne. "King Darius, this new law will strengthen the power of the new empire in Babylon. You have come to this kingdom a stranger. But with this law all peoples will feel bound closer to you. They will worship you; they will adore you!"

Darius settled himself contentedly in his chair. *Perhaps what Abbad said was true.* "What exactly is this law?"

"WHAT EXACTLY IS THIS LAW?"

"Simply this, O King: Anyone who prays to any god or man except to you during the next thirty days will be thrown into the lions' den," said Tobruk, bowing again. "King Darius, issue the decree and put it in writing so that it cannot be changed, according to the laws of the Medes and Persians." He then handed the papyrus to the king.

Without further discussion, King Darius placed his official seal on the law.

Tobruk had made a special point of mentioning the laws of the Medes and Persians for a reason. Unlike the laws of the Babylonians, the laws of the Medes and Persians could not be reversed, even by the king himself. *Daniel will not control this kingdom,* Tobruk thought to himself, smiling slyly. *No one can escape ferocious lions, especially hungry ones.*

The lions of Mesopotamia, the region that

NO ONE CAN ESCAPE FEROCIOUS LIONS.

included Babylon, were prized and feared. Kings were known to hunt them for sport, but lions were also used to kill criminals. In Persia, and now Babylon, lions were even kept and fed in special parks, to be used whenever the situation arose.

Now the situation had arisen, according to this scheming group of presidents and satraps, and all they had to do was catch Daniel in the act of praying.

Daniel was reading in his room in the palace when he was interrupted by several soft knocks on the door. Slipping into his sandals, he made his way slowly to answer. He knew who it was, after all, or he had it narrowed down to three possibilities.

"Mishael, come in, come in. Shall I have some tea prepared for us?"

"No, I cannot stay long today. I have heard some news that is, well. . . ."

KINGS WERE KNOWN TO HUNT LIONS FOR SPORT.

"Please, tell me: Look what we have been through all these years!"

"You are right, of course. A servant just brought me word that King Darius has signed a most unusual law, a law written by all the presidents and satraps, but clearly not by you."

"What kind of law?" Daniel had suddenly become curious and his cloudy blue eyes crinkled at the corners.

Mishael gave him all the details, then hugged him as he left. "Daniel, you do have a choice. Be careful, my friend."

As Daniel sat alone, he considered his "choices," such as they were. He could stop praying for thirty days, or he could hide while praying, making sure no one saw him. Or he could continue as he always had, praying three times a day, gazing through his window open to the west, to Jerusalem.

The choice was not hard for Daniel.

THE CHOICE WAS NOT HARD FOR DANIEL.

And so he continued praying, just as he had for almost eighty years, unaware of who might be watching him. A few days later, the presidents and satraps had all the evidence they needed against Daniel. They had seen him praying to his God, and they had listened to his prayer:

"O God, You who are Most High in heaven, please help me to be strong, and to never stop worshipping You. For You alone are my God."

King Darius was deep in thought when the same group of presidents and satraps approached him. The king opened his eyes and looked straight into their overeager faces. "Well, what is it? What is so important that you disturb my thinking?"

"Did you not issue a decree just days ago, O King, a law that all must worship only you for the next thirty days or risk being thrown into the lions' den?" Abbad asked bravely, all the while knowing the answer.

"O GOD, YOU WHO ARE MOST HIGH IN HEAVEN, PLEASE HELP ME TO BE STRONG."

"Of course! And you were all there, as I recall. The law still stands, a law that even I cannot change." About to lose his patience, the king swatted violently at a bug on the arm of his chair.

"I am sorry to report, O King, that Daniel—he that is to oversee this kingdom—pays no attention to you or to the law you put in writing," Tobruk continued, then paused to make sure the king was listening. "Daniel still prays three times a day to his God!"

The king stared at the men before him, but his eyes were not focused on any of them. His mouth opened slightly and beads of perspiration began to appear on his forehead. "Be gone, all of you! I need to be alone," Darius declared.

As the men scattered out of the king's chambers, Darius put his head in his hands. *How could I have been so foolish to sign such a law?* he thought desperately. *Daniel is a fine man, a man full of wisdom, a man who does not deserve*

THE KING STARED AT THE MEN BEFORE HIM.

to die. And now I have sentenced him to the lions' den!

Raising his hands to the tiled ceiling, Darius yelled out loud, "I must do something! There must be some way I can save Daniel—and I only have until sundown." Pacing back and forth, he suddenly stopped in his tracks. "Quick, send in my legal advisers!" he ordered a servant.

But as sundown approached the king was no closer to finding a way out of the lions' den for Daniel. A decree such as this, issued according to the laws of the Medes and Persians, had no room for exceptions.

"Bring Daniel to me," the king said sadly, his voice barely above a whisper.

As Daniel was led into the king's chambers, he knew the time had come for his faith to be tested again. Yet unlike King Darius, whose eyes were red and robes twisted around his body, Daniel appeared calm and strong.

"BRING DANIEL TO ME," THE KING SAID SADLY.

"Daniel, today I order you thrown into the lions' den for disobeying the law of the empire. May your God, whom you serve continually, rescue you!"

And at that the tall, quiet, white-haired gentleman with the wise eyes was led away, closer and closer to the earthshaking bellows of the hungry beasts.

"DANIEL, TODAY I ORDER YOU THROWN INTO THE LION'S DEN."

A MASSIVE STONE WAS THEN ROLLED IN FRONT OF THE MOUTH OF THE DEN.

10

Terrified by the roars, the king's guards didn't want to get too close to the lions' den themselves. And although Daniel was not holding on to them or showing any fear, still they gave him a mighty push, and backed away quickly.

Following the king's orders, a massive stone was then rolled in front of the mouth of the den and placed over the opening. "There's no chance an old guy like that would escape anyway," one guard said to another.

The other guard nodded his agreement. "If Daniel lasts one minute in there, I'd be surprised!"

Finally, the king arrived and placed his official seal on the stone, applied with wax and his own signet ring, as well as the rings of the presidents and satraps, who were only too happy to be there.

When King Darius returned to his palace later, he hardly looked like the king that he was. Not only were his eyes still red and his robes twisted and falling off his shoulders, but he shuffled his feet and mumbled to himself. Seeing his troubled condition, his personal servants became terribly worried.

"King Darius, the chefs have prepared your favorite dishes for tonight. Simply give the word and the table will be set," one servant began.

THE KING PLACED HIS OFFICIAL SEAL ON THE STONE.

"King Darius, the jugglers and dancers from Persia are here, by your special request. Let me call them in to entertain you before dinner," another servant offered.

"King Darius, let me prepare a bath for you. I have laid out on your bed your softest robes," yet another said, a pleading look on his face.

But to all these requests, the king said nothing. And then he stumbled off to his rooms for the night.

At the same time that King Darius was not acting like himself, Daniel was also in a curious situation. He knew he should be afraid—here he was, in the middle of the night, surrounded by heavily muscled beasts, with no hope of human rescue—but he felt strangely at peace. Truly, God had saved his life again.

Earlier that evening when he had been thrown down into the den, the shock of his fall caused him to pass out briefly. When he awakened there

DANIEL WAS SURROUNDED BY HEAVILY MUSCLED BEASTS.

were several lions sniffing him, their whiskers giving him goosebumps.

Rather than tearing him apart with their bone-crushing jaws, the lions merely seemed to be interested in who he was. Upon realizing that he was completely harmless—and without many teeth!—they left him alone, retreating to an opposite corner of the den.

Amazed at the lions, Daniel looked up only to discover that he was not alone. A few yards away stood a shining being clothed in white, an angel sent from God. As if to answer the question in Daniel's mind, the angel approached a lion and placed its hands on the animal's mouth, and then disappeared from the den.

At that moment Daniel knew, as if he had not fully realized this before. Lying face down in the den, Daniel thanked God over and over again for such a miracle.

All light had left the den by this time, so

A FEW YARDS AWAY STOOD A SHINING BEING...

Daniel curled up in a corner and tried to sleep. But before sleep claimed him, he had one final thought: King Darius is in for the surprise of his life in the morning.

For King Darius, the night was far from restful. After tossing and turning, and pacing around his bed countless times, the king threw on his robes at the first sign of sunrise. Startling his servants who waited outside his rooms, Darius raced to the lions' den. But instead of the usual roars, silence greeted the king.

When he came near the den, Darius cried out hoarsely, "Daniel, Daniel! Has your God, whom you serve continually, been able to rescue you from the lions?" Tears escaped from his eyes, following the lines down his cheeks and running off his chin.

At that moment, the king heard a voice he thought he'd never hear again—Daniel was alive! "O King, live forever!" Daniel's voice

"O KING, LIVE FOREVER!"

was strong and clear. "My God sent His angel and he shut the mouths of the lions. Do not worry, King Darius. The lions have not hurt me at all. I was found innocent in God's sight, and I have done nothing wrong before you either."

Immediately King Darius gave the order to have the stone removed and Daniel lifted out of the lions' den. When he saw him, the king raced to his side, placing his hands on Daniel's shoulders.

"Look at you, my trusted friend. There is not a scratch on your body and even your garments have not been ripped," Darius declared. "You have surely trusted in your God, and your God has delivered you from certain death!"

Then, turning to his guards, Darius gave a most gruesome order. He ordered those presidents and satraps who had plotted against Daniel—Tobruk, Abbad, and the rest—to be thrown themselves into the lions' den. According to the laws of

"THE LIONS HAVE NOT HURT ME AT ALL."

Persia, the families of these men would be thrown into the den as well.

As Daniel and the king made their way back to the palace, the cries of those sentenced to death could be heard, for the lions *were* eating them.

Days later, King Darius called for his scribes to come to his chambers. With papyrus in hand they arrived, and began to record a new law for the king. In the words of Darius, this new decree would be sent to "all the peoples, nations, and men of every language throughout the land," that is, the Medo-Persian empire.

"May you prosper greatly!" the king began to dictate. "I issue a decree that in every part of my kingdom, people must fear and worship the God of Daniel. For He is the living God and He endures forever; His kingdom will not be destroyed and will never end. He rescues and He saves; He performs signs and wonders in the heavens and on the earth."

AS DANIEL AND THE KING MADE THEIR WAY BACK TO THE PALACE,
THE CRIES OF THOSE SENTENCED TO DEATH COULD BE HEARD.

Daniel himself smiled when he read the final sentence. In just a few words, King Darius had learned the power of faith. The king had written, "God has rescued Daniel from the power of the lions."

Such a decree had been a long time coming, especially for Jews like Daniel, Mishael, Hananiah, and Azariah. In so many words, King Darius had now decreed that it was acceptable for Jews to worship their God in any part of the new empire. From this day on, Jews would never be forced to bow down to a golden statue. From this day on, their God would be treated with respect.

Daniel was promptly installed in his new position as chief officer of Babylon, overseeing all one hundred twenty satraps and three presidents. For the next three years, Daniel would serve under Darius and Cyrus the Great, offering his usual wisdom, all in the name of El Elyon, the Most High God.

KING DARIUS HAD LEARNED THE POWER OF FAITH.

Daniel would stay in Babylon, but for other Jews, the time had come to return to Judah, and to their homes in Jerusalem.

DANIEL WOULD STAY IN BABYLON.

DANIEL WALKED SLOWLY DOWN THE WIDE BOULEVARDS OF THE CITY....

11

Dusk was settling on Babylon, that time of day when it seems all buildings and streets are bathed in blue. As Daniel walked slowly down the wide boulevards of the city, he felt the beauty of the moment. But his heart was heavy and sad.

He was taking his time reaching his destination, stopping to greet many people, partly because he did not want this evening to end. He was on his way, after all, to the home of

Hananiah and his family. Mishael and Azariah would be there, too, along with many children, grandchildren, and yes, great-grandchildren.

There would be more food than he could possibly eat, more stories than he could remember to tell, and more reasons to laugh than he had ever found before. And there would be countless pauses when all he would want to do was cry.

In this year of 538 B.C., King Darius had declared that all Jews who wanted to could begin returning to their homeland, to Jerusalem. Daniel, being single and with an esteemed position in the government, felt he could not leave. God's work in Babylon was not finished; he was sure of that.

But his dear friends, after praying all these years facing Jerusalem, could not pass up this opportunity. They were leaving the next day, with their large families in tow, on a journey they had never stopped dreaming about. Their caravans

KING DARIUS HAD DECLARED THAT ALL JEWS COULD BEGIN RETURNING TO THEIR HOMELANDS.

were waiting outside the Ishtar Gate for their departure at first light.

Just before he reached the door to Hananiah's house, Daniel patted the pocket of his robe. *Yes, it is there,* he thought gratefully. *I have not forgotten.*

Hananiah's home was decorated for a festive party, even though all the family belongings had been packed. Candles borrowed from friends and neighbors flickered in their holders on make-shift tables, their flames streaming because of the constant commotion in the rooms. Flowers in vases were in all corners, while above, silk fabric of many colors was hung like streamers across the ceilings, swooping down at points to grace the heads of the taller guests.

As soon as he walked in the door, Daniel became the center of attention. His friends hugged him again and again, and when he looked into their eyes he saw they were filled with tears. How

AS SOON AS HE WALKED IN THE DOOR,
DANIEL BECAME THE CENTER OF ATTENTION.

would he ever make it through this evening? How could he say goodbye to the best friends he had ever had?

Later, after several platefuls of delicacies and several rounds of favorite songs, Daniel motioned for his friends to follow him.

With a candle held in one hand, Daniel led Mishael, Hananiah, and Azariah into the garden, directly behind the house. His friends watched with curiosity as Daniel fumbled in his pocket for a minute. "A few words for your journey," he said as he opened his hand to reveal a worn piece of papyrus.

"Shall we guess what it is? You know, Daniel, my eyes aren't very good," Mishael said.

"Is it a riddle? The answer to a dream I never had?" Azariah was always one for jokes.

Hananiah then spoke up. "No, no, this is something serious. I can tell by the look in Daniel's eyes. He's been planning this for a long time."

HOW COULD HE SAY GOODBYE?

Daniel cleared his throat. "You really don't remember? There we were, spending our first day in Nebuchadnezzar's palace, trying to learn that confusing alphabet. . . ."

"Of course!" cried Mishael. "Our names—you wrote what our names meant in Hebrew so that we would never forget. Let me see. . .Mishael, 'who is comparable to God?' There is surely no other god but God. Remember the first time we were almost killed?"

"Only God could interpret the king's dream in time to save us," Azariah added. "Azariah, 'whom God helps.' Only God could give us strength to survive on water and vegetables. God knew that we needed His strength, the strength to follow the faith of our families."

"And my name, Hananiah, 'whom God hath favored.' I think of that meaning and I am transported back to the fiery furnace. Not a hair on our bodies was burned, my friends, imagine that!

"OUR NAMES... YOU WROTE WHAT OUR NAMES MEANT IN HEBREW."

And our robes did not even smell of a roaring fire," Hananiah remembered. "Yes, God favored us then, and He has favored us now. We will see Jerusalem again."

"And your name, Daniel?" Mishael then asked.

"Yes, 'God is my judge' and I answer only to Him. And that has made a difference here in Babylon, an empire that once worshipped only gods of stone and metal. Because I answer only to Him, God gave me the power to show Nebuchadnezzar —yes, and Belshazzar, too—that there is only one God. And God gave me the strength to continue praying to Him, even though I faced death in the lions' den. When you answer only to God, you can do amazing things. You simply need to have faith."

Daniel paused to catch his breath. Then, tearing the papyrus into three pieces, he handed his friends their "names." "When you reach Jerusalem, no one will know you as Shadrach,

"YES, 'GOD IS MY JUDGE' AND I ANSWER ONLY TO HIM."

Meshach, and Abednego. Godspeed, my friends."

And turning his back on them, Daniel returned to the house to offer his goodbyes, and then headed out into the night toward home.

"GODSPEED, MY FRIENDS."

Reference Notes

Chapter 3, page 50

1. Unlike those in the king's chambers in 602 B.C., you can tell which kingdoms represented what metals in King Nebuchadnezzar's dream. The silver chest and arms was the world empire of Medo-Persia, the bronze stomach and thighs represent Greece and the Macedonia of Alexander the Great, and the iron legs are the great Roman Empire that was in power when Jesus was born on earth. The feet and toes of iron and clay, or the ten kings, have yet to come into power, but will do so before Jesus comes a second time. Someday Jesus will establish His perfect kingdom on earth—in other words, the rock not cut by human hands.

Chapter 4, page 64

2. No record is given of Daniel's whereabouts that day. He may have been away from the city of Babylon on business for the king.

Page 78

3. King Nebuchadnezzar had no idea how right he was when he said the fourth man in the furnace was "a son of the gods" or, as some Bibles state, "a Son of God." Many Bible scholars say that Jesus Christ, the Son of God, who would not be born on earth for more than six hundred years, was in the furnace with Shadrach, Meshach, and Abednego. The reason is found in Isaiah 43:2 (NKJV): "I will be with you. . .when you walk through the fire, you shall not be burned, nor shall the flames scorch you." The Old Testament foretold many things about Jesus, all of which Jesus has done or will do.

AWESOME BOOKS FOR KIDS!

The Young Reader's Christian Library
Action, Adventure, and Fun Reading!

This series for young readers ages 8 to 12 is action-packed, fast-paced, and Christ-centered! With exciting illustrations on every other page following the text, kids won't be able to put these books down! Over 100 illustrations per book. All books are paperbound. The unique size (4 ³¹/₁₆" x 5 ³¹/₄₈") makes these books easy to take anywhere!

A Great Selection to Satisfy All Kids!

Abraham Lincoln	Heidi	Pollyanna
Ben-Hur	Hudson Taylor	Prudence of Plymouth
Billy Graham	In His Steps	Plantation
Billy Sunday	Jesus	Robinson Crusoe
Christopher Columbus	Joseph	Roger Williams
Corrie ten Boom	Lydia	Ruth
David Brainerd	Miriam	Samuel Morris
David Livingstone	Moses	The Swiss Family
Deborah	Paul	Robinson
Elijah	Peter	Taming the Land
Esther	The Pilgrim's Progress	Thunder in the Valley
Florence Nightingale	Pocahontas	Wagons West